Creatures from the Mind of the Engineer

Robert Harbison

Creatures from the Mind of the Engineer

The Architecture of Santiago Calatrava

With Photographs by

Paolo Rosselli

Design: Quim Nolla, Typographer

Edited by: Anthony Tischhauser

Production Assistant: Daniel N. Barceló

Typesetting: Grafitex SA

Photolithographs: Teknocrom

ISBN 3-7608-8083-2

Printed in Switzerland

Santiago Calatrava is a Spanish architect who has operated from Switzerland for the first ten years of his practising life. As a consequence, a high proportion of his early work exists within a narrow radius of Zurich where his sole office was until 1989. ■ The Swiss engineering tradition drew him in the first place, and his first important projects were flamboyant structural adjuncts (roofs, canopies) to other designers' unsensational fabrics. He is a good test case for determining how engineering enters into and becomes architecture, and one can spend a long time unravelling the complicated hybrid of his imagination, where rational calculation and strong dramatic, even pictorial, impulses meet. The move to Switzerland could signify a wish to give two contending forces their due —the desire to express and understand structure with skeletal clarity and the desire to create enormous and impinging creatures. At its best the work caters richly to intellect, senses and emotion at once and is neither as cold as some English High Tech nor as lurid as Gaudí.

Natural Sources

■ In Calatrava the animation which transforms the building from neutral technical experiment to impinging presence as of a gigantic being is wholesomely subliminal. It is by no means obligatory to see the upper gallery of Stadelhofen station in Zurich as a row of spiders, or the platform supports as straining limbs. Calatrava seems to push forms close to the edge where they would lose their resemblance to any everyday model. It is surprising that the little pea-head of the lamp looks like a head any more or its distended leg like plausible anatomy. ■ I don't know whether this particular variation on an organic theme is fruit of long study or sudden understanding. But it seems obvious that most of Calatrava's templates or avatars for structures in general are organic, and furthermore that they come from a particular

Stadelhofen Station→) 1

2 (←Table lamp

corner of organic form. The great stimulus and inspiration to this architect in the natural world is bones and their articulation into the machines which underlie the flesh, organs and connective tissue of complex animals. ■ Wings, so prominent among his most striking roofs, for railway stations and airports, are really a sub-department of skeletal articulation. They are conceived as bony webs on which a fabric or covering is stretched. ■ The great interest in Calatrava's buildings lies not, however, in uncovering the organic analogues, but in seeing how effectively structures and materials have been distanced from petty resemblance, so that the new organism, architecture, though drawing on our feelings about bringing our own muscles and bones into use, offers an unheard of hybrid, to inhabit which requires new thinking about how things move, how weights are lifted and pressures resisted. ■ Up till now, Calatrava's commissions have mostly been connected with industry, transport and various "functional" devices. In part this fulfils an old law of inertia – you are asked to do it because people know you have done it before. He expresses impatience with being typecast this way, but there is a good reason (as well as the bad one noted above) for it, though, as we shall see, it is almost the opposite of the popular notion that he is an engineer rather than an architect. On the contrary, it is that he has found a freedom of expression in these supposedly limited building types – bridges, stations, bus shelters, entrance canopies – which it will be harder to contrive in more stolidly enclosed spaces.

A Rift in the City

■ Unlikely as it sounds, the messy, open-ended and conflicting features of the Stadelhofen site and brief appear in retrospect to have supplied ideal stimulus to Calatrava's structural inventiveness and wit. The site is a large rent or rupture in the fabric of the city caused by the overlay of remnants of the old system of city walls and an intrusive but brief eruption of railway tracks above ground. ■ The plot both slopes and curves along more than one axis. An abrupt change of level from east to west, a gentle incline and then decline from north to south, and a sharp lateral curve in the tracks the whole way across the site add up to a geometrical nightmare or, as it turned out, a series of spatial opportunities. ■ Other architect's proposals suggested roofing the whole unsightly wound over and trying to make the above ground bits look like normal parts of the city, while underneath lay the infernal or at least dark world of the railway. ■ Calatrava's solution, on the contrary, looks like a laying bare rather than a covering up. Instead of hiding the trains he dramatizes their passage. Instead of smoothing out the inequalities he roughens or brings them forth. So the downward slope is brought to life in a diverse series of bridges.

"Bridges"

■The bridge is a notion and a form which means a great deal in Calatrava's work, more than in that of any other current practitioner, one is tempted to say. Among other things, he uses bridges to make large geometrical and structural problems accessible to individual perception: His bridges (in the normal sense of the word) are often distinguished by unusual solicitude for the pedestrian, for the person, that is, in a position to experience the bridge slowly and contemplatively. The thing about a bridge, of course, is that one can't tell much about the spirit in which it is being used at any moment. After it performs its function of shortening or simplifying a journey, what, if anything, is left? Ordinarily, not a lot, but Calatrava's notion of the form is that the designer can interest the user in the struggle to resolve the forces at work in these constructions. So enormous elements are push-

1 (–Stadelhofen Station, Zurich, 1983-1990. Promenade.

2 (–Table lamp. 1990. Prototype.

3 (–Stadelhofen Station. Underside of promenade.

4 (–Stadelhofen Station.

KIOSK

5 (–Stadelhofen Station. Falken footbridge.

(– Bach de Roda Bridge. Barcelona. 1984-1987.

7 (– Bâch de Roda Bridge.

8 (–Stadelhofen Station. Olga footbridge.

9 (– "9th October" Bridge. Valencia. 1986-1988. Pedestrian underpass.

(–Montjuic Standard lamp. 1989.

11 – Stadelhofen Station. Entry to sub-terranian level.

ed out of the easiest, most symmetrical alignments to show the move-
5 (– Stadelhofen Station
ment of thought involved in even the most stable arrangements. ■ The
pedestrian bridges at Stadelhofen are a generally more playful affair
Alamillo Bridge –) 33
than the large road bridges. This does not mean they are simpler; if any-
46 (– Bach de de Roda Bridge
Lusitania Bridge –) 34
thing there is more superficial complexity here. Or perhaps this impres-
9 (– "9th October" Bridge
sion arises from bringing various solutions to similar problems together
in a short space. ■ Calatrava has apparently described the whole project
as a collection of bridges. This is not as fanciful as it initially sounds.
First of all, there are the four different routes spanning the gap between
upper promenade and lower platform at the level of the large open square
Stadelhofen Station –) 4 11
to the west. Then there are the diverse curved canopies which run the
length of the railway's appearance above ground. The inner one of these
appears to carry the open promenade above, making it in effect a long
bridge which has partly collapsed and ended up leaning against the rear
wall. ■ More than this, the whole complex fulfills the spirit of bridges in
Stadelhofen Station –) 1
being so demonstratively "unclothed". Once one is past the back bound-
ary of the site, there is very little wall or cladding. It is like an anatomy
lesson where one has already penetrated past soft outer layers to
essential inner workings. ■ At the same time, of course, the elements
are far from simple or basic. Not that there aren't strong family resem-
blances among forms and reduced variety in the materials. But one great
key to Calatrava's practice here is an extremely unclassical desire for
individual solutions at every stage. Stadelhofen absolutely teems with
simple problems approached freshly, and new answers to what most of
us regarded as no question (or not an interesting question) at all.

A Railing and Gaudí

■ The smallest example is the most revealing —
the railing of the upper promenade consists of waist-high horizontal

segments, approximately two metres long, which belly forward. The Stadelhofen Station-)4 space beneath each segment is closed by two mesh grids in fairly rigid frames. As he likes to do, Calatrava has kept these a short distance from the side and top members to which they are bolted. And, most important, he has given them a slight twist in taking them from the front to the back of the railing's curve. This is more complicated to describe than to see: the result is a kind of optical illusion. Grids which are originally simple rectangles now look like strangely distorted four-sided forms plunging downward. ■ It is one of those moments, of which there are not many, when Calatrava reminds us of Gaudí, extracting oddity from normality and making puzzles for perception out of an unremarkable fact about how things behave. On his general relation to Gaudí one could say it is not readily apparent, that there isn't much superficial resemblance, but that in certain deep patterns of thought or temperament the kinship is real. ■ It could be sketched quickly like this: both these designers enjoy making rigid materials look flexible and active, and both share with Viollet le Duc a liking for improbable clashes between materials — so, metal and masonry (or concrete) are not harmonized but brought into fruitful conflict. Rather one should perhaps say that it is recognized that the natures and capacities of the two materials are so different that they should not be assimilated to a single formal vocabulary. So the diversity remains in the final design, as the harsh play of metal against stone in the balconies and entrances of Casa Mila, or of metal bones against concrete flesh at Stadelhofen.

A Stair and Viollet le Duc

■ I have never understood some of Viollet's most Stadelhofen Station-)8 famous fantasies so well as I did looking at the northern most of Calatrava's bridges there. It is a pedestrian overpass that climbs across in

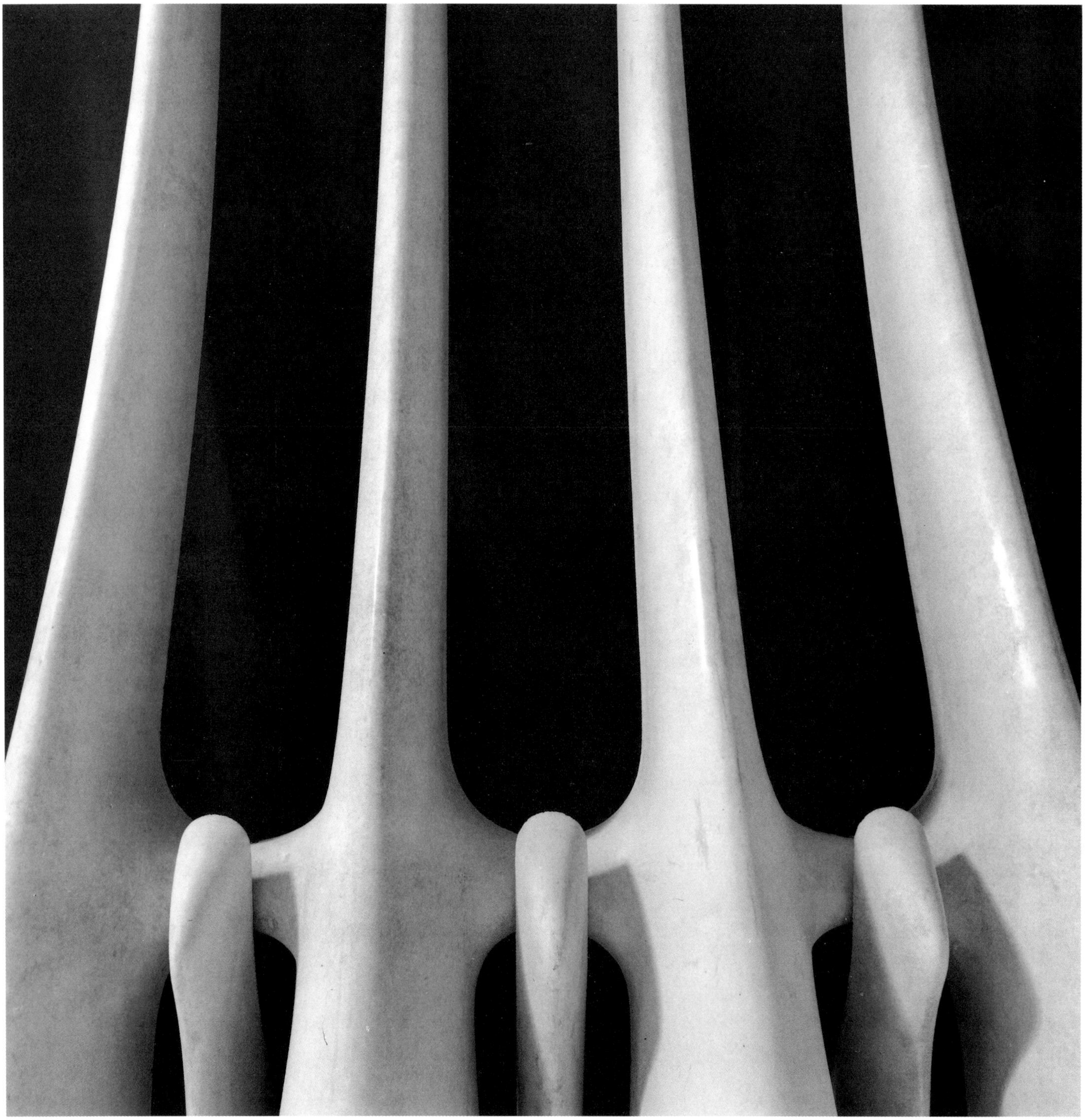

Concrete Pavillion. Swissbau (Swiss Building Fair). Basel. 1989. Individual mobile ribs.

13 (–Concrete Pavillion, Swissbau.

 (-Concrete Pavillion. Swissbau.

15 (–Concrete Pavillion, Swissbau.

front of a tunnel opening, and which needs a stair at one end and not at the other. These inequalities draw forth from the architect exuberant, eccentric imbalances which some probably find wilful and disquieting, while to others they are the high points of the work. ■ Here the single fulcrum is thrown far to one side. One of the main members rising from it is short and straight, the other long and curved, starting at the same angle, which quickly becomes flatter. And then this inequality is, as it were, emphasized with a black pencil — triangular braces between support and walkway shrink as the metal members rise. It is a comical series, as though someone is being squeezed out of a space. There's an underlying seriousness in the plain contrast of off-black metal against off-white concrete, of articulate structure against uncommunicative wall and walkway. ■ It illuminates Viollet's metal-masonry hybrids by suggesting that their power lies precisely in their unresolved quality. There is no way this disparity can really be bridged, and one can reap a kind of energy from admitting the split and assigning starkly different rôles to the two players. So one doesn't seek accommodations but exacerbations: meetings between materials are made abrupt, not gentle. The downward forces are focussed on one point, a huge half-buried ball joint which expresses the maximum of movement and change at the point where the layman expects to be reassured that all is safely inert and will never move. ■ Somewhat at odds with this clear visibility of forces is the feeling that all the metal here constitutes a complete separable mechanism which could be removed, at least in the imagination. Here is a point of contact with Viollet: his proposals were demonstrations or diagrams, almost teaching tools, designed to show how one might initiate a process of innovation. Thus, there is a special point in keeping the new visually distinct from the old. ■ In Calatrava's case the easy observability of structure, which has been interpreted occasionally as a kind of showing off, reflects a belief that the "science" in structures can be more directly translated into general enjoyment than is usually thought, an enjoyment which arises from understanding, perhaps not even consciously, how the design works.

Steel as Bone, Concrete as Bone

■ At Stadelhofen, concrete and steel correspond broadly to flesh and bone, but also represent an underlying consistency which supports or makes tolerable an extreme latitude and variety in the forms. The materials are clear opposites — almost black and almost white, resistant and absorbent, hard and soft, "uncoloured" and therefore in some sense natural. ■ But what is natural? Bone itself in the human skeleton is put through some very odd paces. The thinness to which it is stretched looks highly improbable at times. Viewed aesthetically, as a formal solution the skeleton shows a high tolerance of inconsistency. ■ So on another occasion Calatrava decides to make a delicate moving structure like a fine-boned wing out of arched concrete fingers which weigh 1.2 tons each. This is in some sense a highly unnatural use of the material. It has been given an exquisite finish, like pearly bone, not by polishing but by extreme precision in molding and mixture of constituents, but it is nonetheless unnerving to find such massive elements in rhythmic flux over your head. It is one of those feats one feels was spurred on by its inherent improbability. ■ Does it represent an extension of the possibilities of construction in concrete? It was after all sponsored by the industry and housed their exhibit at the Swissbau in Basel in 1989. Or is it simply a freak showing something "possible" in the sense it could happen, but only once, because it makes people uncomfortable?

Concrete Pavillion→) 12-15

Stadelhofen Station. Sub-terranian shopping arcade.

17 Stadelhofen Station.

Stadelhofen Station.

Dynamism in Architecture

■ That moving roof is probably the most vividly literal bit of dynamism in Calatrava's work to date. But it is a theme which ramifies far beyond the literal. At Stadelhofen the trains are part of the composition. In the great nineteenth-century stations, smoke, noise and movement bring a matter-of-fact architecture to life. ■ At Stadelhofen it is more self-conscious. Piers both lean and sway. Brack-

3 4(-Stadelhofen Station

ets thrust downward, echoing this tense activity. Here, in miniature, and inverted like one of Gaudí's suspended models, the same forces are depicted over again, now a motif rather than a functioning element. Except that it is very satisfying that these brackets carry the power lines which feed the trains and thus sponsor the noisiest movement in this environ-

3(-Stadelhofen Station

ment. ■ Those leaning supports on the inner platform are indeed bewitching shapes. It appears that there's a kind of perspective distortion looking down the row of them. They seem to lean not only back but sideways. Later we learn that the floor slopes too, and the middle of the platform is higher than the ends. So the piers are slightly rayed out like the spokes of a wheel to accommodate this inequality. It was thought their greater backward tilt would disguise the other deviation from true verticality, but it doesn't do so completely, and at some moments you have a sense of a world careening almost violently away from you. The essential point is that Calatrava has set up a force-field in which aber-

Stadelhofen Station-) 16-19

rations can make positive contributions. ■ There is a whole other world below ground here, which wasn't part of the original brief, which grew more complex in a staged way that the architect's mode of working could fruitfully accommodate. This underworld is a shopping centre in a curved tunnel where powerful constraints squeeze the space in both directions. Enormous weights overhead; a high water table underfoot — so you are left with what might have been an oppressively low corridor and the world's greatest overdose of concrete. Calatrava set about it very rigorously, refusing to cover any of the concrete and finding lightness in a determined avoidance of straight lines and right angles, clever use of artificial light, and some very welcome shafts of daylight. ■ The sinuous passage, with huge forms at the entrances suggesting whale's flukes, is like a great intestine. The tunnel as an idea is similar but opposite to the bridge, a ponderous hollowing as against a light spanning; imprisonment against flight, but both of them kinds of contrived route which violate a natural order, primal assertions of human power. At Stadelhofen there is a final exhilarating claim for *building* in the contrast between the two worlds, above and below. ■ No discussion of dynamism in Calatrava's work would be complete without mention of one of his most famous and freakish designs, a row of three warehouse doors at Coesfeld in Germany. They occur in a building which taken as a whole seems a not overly expressive box. They are composed of many relatively narrow vertical slats, which give a pleasing, almost graphic texture to the surface. Only minimal indication is given that these devices are specially odd: their lower halves slope gently inward. ■ When the doors are opened, however, a magical transformation occurs, and the flat surface flutters into a curved canopy through the flexing of a beautifully simple joint in each of the vertical segments. The door has vanished or been pulled through into a new reality, a feat made possible by the employment of a self-lubricating alloy which assures that this formidable array of moving parts will not creak or jam but perform its complex gyration without evident struggle. ■ It's a fascinating instance of Calatrava's relation to technology. This device is barely a commentary on what a door is or is not, but rather an extravagant violation of probability. It's essen-

Ernstings Warehouse→ 20-24

mini-laden
ORIENT

–Ernstings Warehouse, Coesfeld, Germany, 1983-1985. Goods entrance with doors raised.

21 – Ernstings Warehouse. Goods entrance with doors closed.

Ernstings Warehouse.

23 (–Ernstings Warehouse.

 (–Ernstings Warehouse.

25 (–Highschool. Wohlen. Switzerland. 1984-1988. Entrance canopy.

–Lucerne Station. 1984-1989. Station hall.

27 (–Highschool, Wohlen. Entrance canopy.

 (–Highschool. Wohlen. Entrance hall.

 –Highschool, Wohlen. Assembly hall.

(—Highschool. Wohlen. Library.

tial; of course, that the mechanism should work, but the overriding priority is to baffle all expectation in the face of the functional type and task. From their nondescript starting point all these metal vanes erupt without provocation or warning into their aberrant arabesques, as if one traversed the space between Norman Foster at his chilliest and Coop Himmelblau at its most disruptive in a few seconds. In these doors Calatrava runs the whole gamut of contemporary fascination with technology, from the coolest to the most impinging mode. The Austrian team might have let the anarchic impulses rage through the whole structure and influence every one of its contours. Calatrava, by contrast, treats the extravagance as an episode which is isolated in a cool surrounding medium like a controlled explosion in the laboratory. Often his strangest ideas seem to be held at arm's length like this. ■ Coop Himmelblau's results look more consistent, at least in a formal sense, but when one thinks what prodigious calculation went to produce these visions of spontaneous outburst, one is puzzled, to say the least. But this is the perennial conundrum posed by certain kinds of emotional excess in architecture, if not in painting, which one can credit more often as truly momentary production. Dynamic, expressive, and in certain ways profoundly irregular — Calatrava's structures can be all of these, but they don't pretend to be lucky hits or to include a significant proportion of accident.

Roofs as Flight

■ At times he has arrived at a sense of the uncanny or unexpected by an odd route — his contribution to a pre-existing or alien structure is so different in spirit it seems an intruder or afterthought. At Wohlen, 25 kilometres west of Zurich, he got the strange opportunity to provide four separate roofs for the local high school, a well-mannered semi-modernist work by Burkhard, Meyer & Steiger. In retrospect it is hard to imagine how this commission arose. What possessed the host to invite the kind of comparison which now exists between the walls and their covering, between the nondescript and the dramatic, between the monotonous and the adventurous, between flat and curved? ■ It is as if, released from many of the responsibilities of the planner and builder, Calatrava is free to concentrate on four versions of flight. He may have been hired as an engineer but he has reported for work as a sculptor. ■ The first "roof" greets one immediately: it is a glazed entrance canopy. Wohlen Highschool→ 25 27 Apparently it fills a perfectly rectangular plot, and its two slopes are determined by a diagonal drawn very simply from one side to the other. But to perception it appears much weirder than this. It seems that two boldly flaring wings are opposed to each other and glued head to foot. The main planes are strongly twisted, and where the inner one meets the wall, a row of wafer-thin humanoid metal supports grow or shrink to express the relation of this formidable but light metal and glass contraption to the stolid enclosure behind. It is ventilated simply by leaving out the glazing where it arches above the vestibule behind. When one steps past the end of the canopy one finds that the central spine is covered by a fifteen-centimetre strip of plexiglass, while on either side rise the great glass vanes, meant to look flimsy but capable of supporting vast weights of settled snow or climbing children. Drain spouts are one of the most amusing details, like the folded rear parts of origami birds. One would like to see this enchanting mathematical puzzle in a violent rainstorm. ■ Next in the sequence of four roofs is one I Wohlen Highschool→ 28 would prefer to leave out, though it makes an essential contribution to understanding Calatrava as a designer. It is the most exquisite of the four, a big circular wooden flower which covers the entrance hall rotunda and shows from the outside of the building as an archaic little lan-

– Alamillo Bridge, Seville, Spain, 1987–1992.

– Alamillo Bridge. Undercroft and Expo'92 portico.

 (– Lusitania Bridge, Merida, Spain, 1988-1991.

35 (– Stadelhofen Station. Tunnel entrance.

"9th October" Bridge. Valencia. Bridge underside.

37 –Lyon Airport Station. Lyon-Satolas, France, 1989–. Platform tunnel.

–Lyon Airport Station. Platform tunnel.

39 —Bach de Roda Bridge. Support and stair underside.

– Bach de Roda Bridge. Support and stair underside.

tern. Its lesson can be left until last. ■ Next comes the library, a contender for most dramatic of the four, and formally the simplest. This
30 31 (– Wohlen Highschool
roof is supported by a single central column and does not touch the walls at any point, except for four little metal spindles which one has to look for in order to see. The roof proper is a large unbroken form in concrete, folded along two axes which emanate from the central column, toward which the concrete swoops down massively, gracefully, like wings or like a great weight. The whole system is alternately exhilarating and menacing: there are sensations of flight around the edges, where much daylight creeps and sidles in through an unbroken band of glazing which closes the space between the curved concrete and a notional remnant of the higher flat ceiling which this room might have been given; but wasn't. ■ Climbing to the balcony full of reading desks you get the strongest sense of the big concrete keel cleaving the space. It intrudes so far into it from this perspective that the spectator is surprised there's room enough left for him. This sheet of concrete forms an overpowering instance of a latecomer arriving in a space and redefining it completely. ■ Although all the walls are white, the ceiling remains unpainted and one can reach up and feel the extremely fine unbroken surface which, through its darker colour and the lighting, remains an under-
Alamillo Bridge –) 33
side, not a sky. In his bridges too we find Calatrava fascinated by the
35 (– Stadelhofen Station
Lusitania Bridge –) 34
situation of being underneath something — underneath, in fact, the
"9th October" Bridge –) 36
whole structure, though it is a realm or an experience which architec-
Bach de Roda Bridge –) 39 45
ture usually disguises or forgets. ■ In this library the idea is unexpectedly welcomed — in the looming concrete form, but also in the overexpressed steel support, vaned as if it has an additional job as a heat diffuser and tapered toward top and bottom like the cartoon of an ancient order. Only when I had inspected a model of this roof from above,

where one sees stiffening ridges meeting at the middle, did it dawn on me that the column is hollow and carries rainwater away. All in all it is one of the architect's most magicianly performances. ■ The last roof covers the aula or assembly hall and consists of canted concrete posts supporting a complex superstructure of simple timber members lightly wiped with paint. Again there is tremendous attention to how it will be lit and thus appear. The light comes from underneath via a sloping clerestory. The structure is independent of the walls, the lower elements standing well free of them like arcades in an aisled church. These are the most exquisite pieces of concrete work in any of the Calatrava projects I have seen, of amazing silky texture and full of sculptural indentations and incisions. Viewed sideways, these piers are strongly humanoid with clear heads and feet, but seen from behind the concrete terminus is a bony knuckle to which the finer wooden bones of the arched wings above are hooked. This wooden structure is one of Calatrava's most harmonious, whose material and lighting make one think of Aalto.

Wohlen Highschool-) 29

Theatrical Excesses

■ Wood is also the most prominent material in the roof we have neglected, the circular one. To me that represents a certain tendency I sometimes detect in this architect pushed too far, a tendency to sinuosity and a kind of curvaceousness which sometimes, though not here, smacks of Art Nouveau or a decadent organicism. ■ An insertion in an old building for the Theatre Tabourettli in Basel exemplifies this tendency best and is therefore illuminating though in some ways it is one of the least satisfactory of Calatrava's works. In most instances his preference is to exploit a limited palette of materials — two or three at most — richly. At Tabourettli, by contrast, he employs a plethora of different substances, including some luxurious in a super-

Tabourettli Theatre-) 41-44

41 (–Tabourettli Theatre, Basel, 1986–1987. Stairhall trusswork.

–Tabourettli Theatre. Staircase.

 –Tabourettli Theatre. Cloakroom and support.

—Tabourettli Theatre. Staircase.

42 44 (– Tabourettli Theatre

ficial or conventional way. ■ The principal idea is undeniably ingenious and amusing – a flamboyant glass and metal stair is inserted in a fairly narrow space, and then used twice – a later passage crosses over, even seems to thread its way through it, and the stair now constitutes a bit of interesting scenery displayed beneath our feet. ■ The whole setting is theatrical in good and bad senses: the metal framework of the stair opens like a giant mouth, at the back of which unfortunately a small cusp seems to play the tonsils. Or piercings form themselves up into a complete but distended mask. These shapes are all in black metal which makes sharp silhouettes, but the rails are chrome, the glass risers are frosted and there are minor eruptions of yellow metal. ■ In the vestibules metal and glass, in bar and theatre much warm wood and blood-red upolstery. Wooden flaps open like lapels from the windows, which when closed resemble large angular crystals. ■ The stair is the best part, but somehow it makes one think of Oscar Wilde and a world of fathomless artifice. It is hard to understand how Calatrava the designer of bridges could also happily adopt the jeweller's approach to materials and form evident not only in the elaborations at Tabourettli but in such other small works as sculpture and furniture. Structural ideas seem masked by the high polish or variegated surface of the materials chosen. There is a strange and off-putting coldness about certain of these works on the most intimate scales, like the ascending sugar cubes in polished granite or marble. ■ But Anthony Tischhauser has rightly observed that formal and statical problems often surface first in the sculptures and turn up only later in bridge designs. It was an eye-opener to go to and see one of the sculptures which had seemed just tricky when table-top size translated into concrete, some fifteen metres high, standing outside the cement plant of Herr Wey who has worked with Calatrava for eight years.

The Rôle of the Model

■ So the luxurious materials *did* conceal an exciting structural device. Maybe all one was asking for was to see the *model* for the sculpture in wood and string. Certainly the model plays a critical rôle in his practise: forms develop as Calatrava draws in pencil on, reshapes and suggests changes in a model. At this point architecture is in a very specific way like sculpture: the right form is in the block, and one adjusts the requirements of what one knows the members must do to the kind of thing one wants them to say. I continue to think the "sculptures" would communicate more authentically if they came dressed in the clothes of workaday models. ■ There are certain other projects which can only enter tangentially here because they have not been built, like the projected completion of the Anglican cathedral in New York or the bridge over the Thames below London. But we need to return from Calatrava the tinkerer to Calatrava the builder of Utopian visions, who sometimes neutralizes his materials in the true spirit of the engineer, impelled to deny reality and invent or project ideal substances which he does not expect or want us to be able to account for. The final stage in a consideration of Calatrava's use of materials is reached in these moments of visionary transcendence.

Utopian Visions

■ So one can legitimately discuss the materials the bridge for London is made of, even though it probably won't be built. It is steel of course, but steel neutralized to a weightless ideal substance simply by painting it white. You couldn't get this effect by painting just any bridge white, though. In this design various elements contribute to the sense of a minimal form of almost percussive force that enables it to sail over the flatland below. ■ Again Calatrava was pushed

50 (– Bach de Roda Bridge

–Bach de Roda Bridge. Pedestrian access stair

– Bach de Roda Bridge.

47 (–Bach de Roda Bridge.

MEGUSA
SEVILLA

–Alamillo Bridge. Pylonbase.

49 (– Alamillo Bridge. Roadbed cantilevers.

50 (–Bach de Roda Bridge. Twin arch.

by circumstance to come up with a design which strains against the edges of credibility. Planes from London City Airport and ships from downriver force the roadway up and the arch down. The result is a horizontal vector which rides very high in the more tightly curved form. Thus it seems on the point of breaking free. Though it is huge, the surrounding proportions make the arch look small, and its great legs feel like a perspective distortion, as if one is seeing it from underneath or misrepresented in a mirror.

De Chirico in Steel and Concrete

■ In some minds at least this design will loom as a permanently embarrassing mirage over the clumsy affair which will usurp its place. In certain ways this design was well calculated for London. It is much less flamboyant than the smaller bridge over a railway cutting in Barcelona, called Bach de Roda after the street it carries. At the outer edge of that bridge is a surprising feature, an exposed stairway in concrete like something in a de Chirico painting, suggesting a thwarted or endless journey. ■ But the line of this stair, so purely expressive, is also the line of the bridge's main support. In Calatrava's designs there is never truly unadulterated mass, even the supports are characterful; and the heaviest members suggest movement, being pierced or inverted so that they portray the pressures acting on them as well as resisting them. ■ At Bach de Roda the great arching curve which starts on the ground in concrete switches to steel halfway up when it reaches the roadway. The coupling where the change occurs is mesmerising; at that point the simplicity of the form is denied by the complexity of the engineering, that is to say by a difficult joint. It is like acknowledged war between the architect and the engineer, one of them bent on denying; the other on exhibiting the difference between these two materials.

45 47 (– Bach de Roda Bridge

7 (– Bach de Roda Bridge

At that moment and precisely at the level of the passing spectator the tension between these two main strands of Calatrava's talent makes an engrossing bit of material drama.

Where Next?

■ Calatrava appears to have reached a turning point. The TGV station now being built at Lyon airport is on a much larger scale than any of the completed projects. Bits of urban re-planning now in the air for the Spandau district in Berlin represent a further quantum leap. In models and drawings Lyon looks very promising, though basically a magnification of the kind of forms we have seen in earlier roofs and pavilions. ■ The urban opportunities at Spandau bristle with much greater promise and menace. Will he be able to intervene structurally in the city, propping here, forcing a passage there, and roofing odd-shaped crevasses he finds in a pre-existing terrain? We have to hope he isn't given blank slates, but problem-sites, partly congested, partly inaccessible, which demand great structural flights in order to become coherent in the first place. We know he won't spend the next ten years putting roofs on other people's buildings, but maybe some of it will go to resurrecting bits of cities so impacted no one else sees any room for exuberance or wit in them at all.

Lyon Airport Station→) 37 38

Robert Harbison, October 1991

Describing an Object. When thinking, of the various horizons I have gradually had to find for an oeuvre that seemed to change continuously as I recorded it, I should say that the concrete world of Santiago Calatrava, the engineer and the architect, has at times suggested and in some cases "dictated" images to me. My constant endeavour to deepen the photographic response has also been an attempt to make it, for others and for myself, more real, or in other words less artistic, less abstract.

Perhaps when we speak of photography's ability to describe an object we ought to admit that this prerogative is not automatic and may break down in the face of certain realities; or to say that every picture, though forming part of a larger work, is an experience in its own right. Or again, this "work", which consists in continually dismantling and reassembling the totality which is the architectural object, so as to get a hold of it and master it, often has an unexpected result; that is why I think that describing an object through photography is in reality "writing" it – I can find no better word – in many different ways. One of these may perhaps prove to be new or simply more adequate; for writing is not exhausting one's knowledge of reality in a sum of impersonal phrases, but leaving things so that this reality remains in a sense a point of contrast in which one feels personally involved.

Paolo Rosselli, November 1991